Born 1943.
Studied briefly at Croydon Art School.
Lived abroad for six years in New Zealand and Canada. Started drawing cartoons, part-time, in 1969 and became full-time freelance in 1972.
Married with one son.

"Ready? They're coming"

PRIVATE EYE

Cartoon Library 4

100 best jokes of

HONEYSETT

A Private Eye Book with André Deutsch · London

Also published in this series:
The 100 best jokes of Michael Heath. Hector Breeze. And Larry.

Published in Great Britain 1974 by
Private Eye Productions Limited, 34 Greek Street, London W1.
In Association with André Deutsch Limited,
105 Great Russell Street, London WC1.

SBN 233 96 563 7.
Some of the following cartoons were drawn for this book.
Most were first seen in Private Eye.
Others appear by kind permission of the Evening Standard
and the Daily Mirror.

Designed by Peter Windett
Printed in Great Britain by A. Wheaton & Company, Exeter.

"I was supposed to have had a sleeper."

"Just trying it out for the kids."

"Now up a bit."

"I see Jones and Philpott haven't got back from the King's Head yet."

HONEYSETT.

TELEVISION CO.
EASY TERMS
BUS STOP
JESUS LOVES YOU
HONEYSETT

"Not another coup!"

"I had to throw you in to clinch the deal."

HONEYSETT

HONEYSETT

"I still think we would have been better off using native porters."

"It's bad enough being de-frocked, without you being proud of it".

"Where the hell have you been?"

"You shouldn't have told her that he's gone to the great pub in the sky."

"He's right, Sid, he's got a preservation order."

"I might be late tonight, dear, I've got a pile of work to get through."

"Sorry to trouble you but this gentleman thinks he left some chewing gum under that seat"

HONEYSETT.

" I know it's a nice day but you don't have to put *all* the tables and chairs outside."

"It's for the Americans, they love to hear their 'Benny Goodman'!"

"I wish you'd stop asking complete strangers why you haven't seen them in church lately."

"This is ridiculous, trying to do the ironing during the commercials."

" Because it was you that forgot the flag, that's why."

"Trust you to forget our anniversary."

"*Two Toad in the 'ole, medium rare.*"

"Morning Mum. What's for breakfast, dinner, tea and supper?"

"You see, I told you we'd hear about nothing else but their holiday in Tahiti."

"I think the governor's being too lenient, letting them still have visitors."

"That's what comes of being reared by wolves"

"No, I don't think so, Hodgekins."

"Yeah, I'll let you know."

"I don't care if you did have a few bits left over!"

"I like to keep the garden looking nice and smart."

"In case anyone should fall into the fish tank."

"For God's sake Harry, let go of the elephant"

"Never missed a works beano yet, has Sir Frank."

"I still say there's a public footpath through here."

"You're right, this is fun."

" Harry hates being pestered by beggars."

"Sorry, it's closed to visitors at feeding time."

HONEYSETT.

SNOD & SNOD SOLICITORS
LAST CHANCE
TO MAKE
A WILL
BEFORE THE
MOTORWAY
HONEYSETT

"It's not him I mind—it's the trouble you have finding a chemist who can fill his prescriptions."

"He wants to know if tea's ready yet"

"Master thinks you're hanging the pheasants for too long."

"It's been there for three months now, perhaps it *has* been dumped."

"He shouldn't have tried to blow them all out."

". . . and of course, a company car"

HONEYSETT

Saying the bogeyman will get him doesn't seem to have much effect these days.

" It's my Book of the Month."

"Now that's what I call spitting."

"That's my TV detector van early warning device."

"It's a start brother. it's a start."

"Dammit Simpson, this is the third time you've let the tortoise escape".

" Old Smithers hasn't changed much, has he ? "

"You and your crazy ideas about saving money on a staircase."

" I am certainly not forming a posse just to look for your cat."

"Anything to get out for a pint."

T MISSION
HONEYSETT.

"Apparently it's a free sample of toothpaste."

"of course, ideally, it should be a tiger's skin."

"Trouble with the car again Mr. Henshaw?"

"Jones, could you crawl into my office for a moment?"

"I know he's an infant prodigy, but at least he could read the paper *after* I've gone to work."

EITHER YOUR FISH GO, OR I DO.
HONEYSETT.

"She'll grow into them."

"We'll let you know. Next please."

"Be reasonable dear, it's hard to break old habits after thirty years in the army"

"They come in to keep warm on cold nights."

"I don't see why he can't remember where he buried them himself."

" Believe me, old boy, it's not at all what it used to be."

"Would you mind if I go ahead of you."

"I think we could have done without his female impersonations for one day, don't you?"

" Right ! Who hasn't been up yet ? "

HONEYSETT.

"He loves to dramatise things."

HONEYSETT

"She's afraid they might re-open the line without telling us."

"This just isn't good enough Nigel - That's the third one you've drowned this week"

"Remember, no visitors after 8.30 p.m. and no baths, except on Saturdays!"

COINS

CLICK!
COINS

"God has also chosen me to speak to you about insurance "

"I'll have a pound of mince and six flies please."

"I enjoy his sermons, I must say."

"We must be crossing the Equator."

"I don't know which is worse—Saturday mornings for kids or Thursday afternoons for pensioners"

HONEYSETT.

"*I'm not having my gun mistaken for a real one.*"

"He says his pools win won't change him, but already he's hired a bloke to put his dog ends behind his ear."

"He's been the same ever since they introduced closed circuit television in the shops."

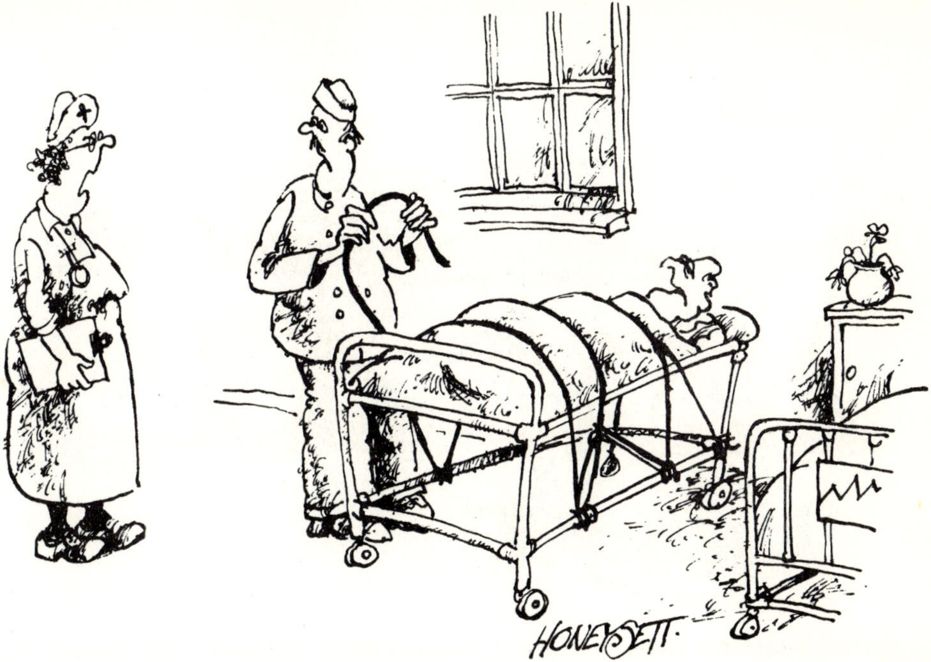

"Yes, well you're a medical orderly now, not a lorry driver "

"Listen, when Big Louis says you're gonna take a ride, don't ask questions, just go!"

"I thought it was only dolphins that did that sort of thing."

"We'd like to see some wardrobes please"